The Simple Way to Start the GF/CF Diet

The Simple Way to Start the GF/CF Diet

An Easy Guide to Implementing the Gluten Free/Casein Free Diet for Your Child with Autism

NATALIE A. KULIG

Our mission is to efficiently provide the world's finest, most comprehensive book publishing service, enabling every author to experience success. To find out how to publish your book, your way, and have it available worldwide, visit us online at www.trafford.com

Trafford rev. 11/17/2009

 www.trafford.com

North America & international
toll-free: 1 888 232 4444 (USA & Canada)
phone: 250 383 6864 ✦ fax: 812 355 4082

You have heard about the Gluten Free/Casein Free (GF/CF) diet helping some children with Autism, but the idea of removing wheat and dairy seems impossible.

This is your easy guide on why the diet may work and recipes and ideas to get started quickly.

The author also gives you a small insight into her life dealing with the Autism Spectrum, along with a little humor and a lot of hope.

To big brother, Zach –
For always understanding

I know God will not give me anything I can't handle. I just wish that He didn't trust me so much.

— Mother Teresa

Please note that there is no double blind placebo study done on whether or not the GF/CF Diet helps with Autistic behavior. This book is based on my own experience with using the GF/CF diet as well as working with a doctor for special blood tests, supplement use and other therapies, including physical therapy, occupational therapy, speech therapy and additional tutoring. No portion of this book should be taken as medical advice.

Preface

Just thinking about beginning the Gluten Free/Casein Free Diet is overwhelming.

I remember first hearing about the diet just shortly after my then 3-year-old daughter was diagnosed with Autism. I read an article by Karyn Seroussi in Parents Magazine (February 2000) about how she cured her son's autism with this Gluten Free/Casein Free Diet. I read it and dismissed it. I was not going to start taking things out of my child's diet without even understanding what this diagnoses meant to my daughter or my family.

And so, my long journey began. Each of us handles the diagnoses of Autism in a different way. At first, it is hard to accept. Then we need to blame someone or something. Then we accept. What we do during this time, however, is critical.

Because I am a researcher by nature, I began my journey the day I received her diagnoses. The team of doctors and therapists that diagnosed her sent me home with handfuls of information, articles and therapy options.

As I read countless medical articles, it was confusing as to what therapies my daughter might need. I had heard about ABA, supplements, occupational therapy and diet treatments. I chose the path of somewhat "alternative" medicine looking to a chiropractor for initial help. I started my journey at a center in Louisville, Kentucky called the Kentuckiana Children's Center. They concentrated on children with special needs. It was at this Center where I learned about many alternative treatments that I believe have profoundly helped my daughter. There are many scientific books out there to help explain the details of how gluten and casein are tolerated, so I have not gone into great detail on the science and etiology of this matter. My intention is to help guide you through some of the information and how to use it. What we do with our children is extremely personal—from how we discipline to what therapies we use. Plus, anyone with a child on the spectrum knows that it is so large, there is no "one size fits all" remedy.

A special note of thanks.....

My journey began 10 years ago, but my daughter's progress has been amazing and I could not have done it without the following people!

Dr. Pat Purcell, East Louisville Pediatrics – she diagnosed Vicky at 2 ½.

First Steps – for pointing me in the right direction.

Lyndon Pre-school, Louisville, KY – to all the specialists and teachers who helped Vicky cope in a school setting with other children.

Dr. Wendy Gallego for helping me start the diet and supplements.

Kentuckiana Children's Center – for their guidance in the diet, and their support in finding alternative ideas to helping her.

Easter Seals of Louisville – For their outstanding help and efforts in speech and occupational therapy.

Dr. John Hicks and Pathways Medical

Back in the Saddle – Hippo Therapy and Tweety the horse – for giving Vicky confidence.

My family and friends who have put up with the tantrums, food difficulties, altering their plans last minute and just plain supporting our family.

Contents

Chapter 1

My Story

Ahh...the sweet smell of baby powder, pink clothes, rattles, dolls and did I mention the screaming? Eight months of colic. "Does she ever stop crying?" my husband asked. Lucky for him, he did not get the first four hours of the day – thank goodness my son was in school – only myself and the neighborhood had to endure the morning screaming fits which stopped as abruptly as they started.

Hold her? Cuddle Her? Rock Her? Adore Her? Not a chance on this planet – I was considering a move to Mars – maybe no one would hear her scream.

Both devastation and relief came with her diagnoses of Autism. For the first three years of her life, I thought that I had to be the worst parent in the world. After having my first child, a boy, who hit his milestones on time or early, how could I have given birth to this sweet little girl who seemed to be so miserable most of the time? I used to watch parents struggle with children screaming in the malls, kicking in the grocery cart and flaying in their strollers. Now, I was the parent of one of "those" kids...and it was not fun to be on this side of the fence.

In 1998, I wrote an article for a local moms group entitled, "Apologies from the Perfect Parent." I used to think all those parents with the misbehaving kids just did not know how to parent their kids. After all, my son could go anywhere or do anything. Was I sorry for ever thinking that way. Now it was my daughter people were staring at and making comments under their breath. When her diagnoses of PDD-NOS came into play, there was a part of me that was slightly relieved. I guess I was not such an awful parent after all. But Autism? Tears streamed down my face. My baby girl had Autism. How was I supposed to feel, what was I supposed to do? I waited 7 years between my children and had three miscarriages during those years. How could this long awaited child, my little girl, MY child have Autism?

The Child Evaluation Center in Louisville was where she received her diagnoses. Her team of evaluators included a medical doctor, a psychologist, a social worker, an occupational therapist, and a physical therapist. After four hours of interviews and evaluations and a 17 page single-spaced typed report, their findings were relayed to us. "It is our impression Victoria presents with a Pervasive Developmental Disorder, manifesting as communication impairments with social communication deficits, diminished imaginative play skills with some repetitive behaviors and desire to be consistent with the diagnoses of the autistic disorder."

In a nutshell, they considered her high functioning – but what exactly did that mean? The team piled high in front of us articles, reference materials, suggestions on how to educate her and a sea of other information. What could they really tell us about her future? Absolutely nothing. Did she have cognitive impairment? Maybe, maybe not. Would she be mainstreamed in her education? The team recommended a jump-start preschool program to see how she would do. They suggested social stories, social training, intensive behavioral intervention, Picture Exchange Communication System, model play, encourage participation in play, facilitate responsiveness to language, and provide occupational therapy. Okay, anyone speak Greek? I had absolutely no idea what any of this meant. I was a marketing manager who had just retired three years previous, to be a stay at home mom. Now they were talking about things I had never heard of.

I felt as if we were stepping out onto a LIFE® game board. Would we roll the dice and make it past the dreaded space you did not want to land on or would we in fact roll those snake eyes and end up paying the price. Before her diagnoses, colic was a major issue and a visit to my pediatrician suggested that it might be her formula causing the colic. So we began the formula roulette. After attempting every formula on the market, we finally settled on some predigested formula (who predigested it, I really can not say I wanted to know). There went the budget, as it was much more expensive than regular formula, but at least the screaming stopped.

I think that was my precursor to the GF/CF diet. I may not have known it then, but that early formula chess game was just my brief introduction into the food web I would be marching into. You see, not only do I have the amazing maze of the GF/CF diet, I live with Type I diabetes, so diets just seem to be my lot in life. Read on to understand a little better on why this may be the right path for you and your child.

Chapter 2

First Steps to Understanding
the Purpose of the Diet.

I believe the first step to implementing the diet is to read Karyn Seroussi's book, *Unraveling the Mystery of Autism and Pervasive Development Disorder, A Mother's Story of Research and Recovery* (Simon and Schuster, 2000). This book will give you the background of all her research and how she uncovered what different foods and their proteins could do to the body.

When I read what gluten and casein could do to the body and mind of a child with Autism it was so surprising. I was also astounded by the affect of apples, bananas and other fruits that contained high amounts of natural phenol sulfates and the opiate-like effect it could have on the brain. I remembered her early days and her colic. I started my daughter on the diet in July of 2000 – she was three years old at the time. The effects were profound. Although I would not go as far as to say the diet cured her, the improvements I saw after only a month or so on the diet gave me hope. Now, almost a teenager, she makes her own food choices and knows what she can and cannot have. I believe that the earlier the diet intervention, the easier time the child will have making this a life long habit.

The first time she emerged from her own little autistic world and asked me to play, I cried. When she looked up at the sky while on vacation, she noted all the "sheep" in the blue sky (the clouds). While we take for granted these small gestures in our normal developing children, we are amazed and rewarded when our children with Autism make these same milestones.

A doctor once explained the diet and why is works in lay terms. Here is a brief synopsis on why the diet works. This is the explanation I use to inform friends, family and school personnel so that they understand WHY my daughter cannot have gluten or casein.

> Your body takes all food it digests in to the stomach. From there, the stomach then breaks down the food proteins into peptides. They are again broken down one more level to amino acids. These amino acids are released into the blood stream so the body utilizes them. In the case of many children with Autism, their bodies have what is called a "leaky gut". This means that the peptides get into the blood stream before they break down into amino acids. The body does not know how to use them and they begin to clog up the body's own system and block neurotransmitters to the brain.

Wheat and dairy proteins seem to be the biggest offenders, although Often, corn and soy may also be culprits; each child is unique. This also explains why, if your child does respond positively to the diet it is as if a fog has lifted and everything becomes clearer.

This was the case with my child. She went from barely speaking words, throwing tantrums and screaming to get what she needed, to speaking in 3-4 word sentences. A year and a half later, she became fully verbal. Today, she is mainstreamed in her class room. She has hopes and dreams of going to college.

She learned many of her first speech patterns through the videos she watched; today she can tell me what she needs. She even knows she has autism and will tell me when the day is a particularly hard day. Autism is a complex condition and no two children on the autistic spectrum are alike. It is my belief that the diet is a good place to start finding answers. Even with many medical doctors waving their hands and discrediting the diet, I still feel it is worth the time and effort. The most important thing is for you to give the diet time to work. Your child may not respond immediately. In my opinion, it is an all or nothing effort – a little milk or a little wheat is a big deal – you must make a commitment.

Now it is time to look into the workings of the diet. Keep in mind that if you decide to do this diet…

- It will be difficult,
- You will make many, many mistakes,
- Depending on the age of your child, you may not see immediate results, it may take weeks or months, or even years,

- Your grocery bill will go up,
- You will become a connoisseur of ingredients you never heard of,
- It will become easier as time goes by,
- And most importantly, it may be the piece of your child's autism puzzle.

That said, let us begin!

Chapter 3

Ingredients

Take Out the Diary!

The first and easiest step is to take out milk and dairy. What should you use instead? Here are some alternatives listed in order of the ones we like best!

- Vance's™ DairiFree™ – Creamy, mild, pleasant flavored non-dairy powder milk made from potatoes. It is rich in calcium and vitamins, low in sugar. Since it is in a powder form, it makes it easy to travel. The best way to make it is a pitcher with an aeration plunger. Measure out the milk, mix with about 1-2 cups of hot water to dissolve the powder quickly and easily, then add the cold water and aerate again to mix well. It keeps up to a week in the refrigerator. They also make a dairy free chocolate version.

- Soy Milk – There are many types of Soy Milk available at your grocery store. When my daughter first started, we had to purchase it at a health food store, now, most major food chains stock a variety of brands. You can purchase refrigerated soy milk in the dairy case – from Original to Vanilla, from

Chocolate to Strawberry. Test which one your child likes best.

- You can also purchase Soy milk in the non-refrigerated health food area as well. These containers are sealed and do not need to be refrigerated until they are opened. This makes it easy to stock up or to use when you travel.

- Soy Silk® is one of our favorite chocolate varieties. For portability, get a good plastic "juice box" container with the straw. There are also some varieties of soy milk in single serve containers.

NOTE: Some children may self-addict to soy products. If you notice that they can't seem to get enough soy milk in a day, you may have eliminate and then reintroduce a cup a day. Watch your child's behavior during this time and see if you notice any differences.

- Rice Milk – You must be very careful in choosing this type of substitute. Some of them carry trace amounts of barley which contain gluten. Read all labels carefully. These also come in juice box form and can be a great carry along drink.

In addition to milk, you must take out the following:

- Yogurt – There are tasty alternatives in your grocer's dairy section – however your best choices are most likely to be found in a Health Food Store.

- Cheese – Unfortunately, in my opinion, there are no good casein free cheeses that taste good. On one occasion, my half-sister who is also a vegetarian, told me about this great soy cheese. She brought it to a party to have my daughter taste it. When I saw the way it melted, I was convinced it had casein in it (this is the dairy protein). She was sure since it said VEGAN that it was safe, but when she got home and checked the label, it did contain casein. My general rule is that if the cheese melts like cheese, it has casein in it. If it doesn't melt, it's probably okay, but won't have much flavor. We have chosen to eliminate it. You should give it a try and see if it matches your child's taste buds.

- Butter - Look for soy spreads, Spectrum® Brand Spread, or Fleishman's® unsalted. Just make sure that there are no butter solids, whey (a dairy by-product), or casein.

- Ice Cream/Non-Dairy Treats – Freeze Pops are a good choice during summer – although loaded with sugar and food color, for a hot summer day, these treats are handy to have in the freezer. Soy Ice Cream is available in vanilla, chocolate and many other flavors, and it is so good that I bet most of you couldn't tell the difference if I served it for dessert. Also look for GF ice cream cones – they look like sugar cones and are delicious.

BEWARE OF SHERBET –Sherbet is not ice cream, but it contains milk solids.

Sometimes it seems that your child with the special diet makes it hard to go out for ice cream for the rest of the family. When heading out to the Dairy Queen®, your GF/CF child can order a dairy free Star! At Culvers® order the summer favorite, Lemon Ice and at Cold Stone Creamery® and other ice cream shops order the dairy free sorbet.

My hope is that some day all ice cream places will carry soy ice cream so that everyone can enjoy the summer outing of going out for ice cream.

After eliminating dairy, you should notice some behavior changes in your child. Maybe they won't rock as much, or maybe they will begin to be more alert, and offer more eye contact. In my daughter's case, we noticed that she didn't flap her hands any more. Keep a log or diary, if you must, to help document the changes that you observe.

Bread – Gluten's biggest friend

Bread is probably the trickiest of all things to eliminate. There are many types of bread on the market: They can be made from rice, soy, quinoa, bean, or a mix of different flours. Some of them taste like stale paper; others are only good if you microwave the slice for 30 seconds. My daughter's favorite is the Rice Sandwich bread made by Kinnikinnick™ Foods. You will find it in the frozen food section your local health food store. I get many GF/CF items directly shipped from Kinnikinnick™ Foods every six weeks, but it still needs to be frozen to be kept fresh. When making sandwiches, I defrost two slices for two minutes and the bread has a good moist texture.

Loaves of bread can be expensive. There are mixes available to help you cut corners and make a homemade loaf. Although you can make them in a bread machine, I recommend mixing the recipe in a bowl and baking in the oven. If you are not a baker at heart, go ahead and use the bread machine, it will still have that homemade taste.

> HINT: Slice the bread with an electric knife to get even, thinner slices and freeze immediately.

> HINT: Whether you bake the bread yourself or buy it ready made, before freezing, separate the slices so that they can be removed slice by slice when frozen. Invest in small freezer bags and individually freeze one or two slices to have them handy to make sandwiches.

There are also different varieties of hot dog and hamburger buns on the market as well. These make summer time barbeques fun for your child on this diet.

Baking

If you are a baker at heart, you should really enjoy the challenge of baking gluten/casein free. I love to bake and find it rewarding when I can come up with a cookie, cake or bread recipe that my daughter gobbles up and her friends can enjoy without knowing it is GF/CF.

If you plan to be a GF/CF baker, the following items are a must have in your kitchen:

> ➢ A good Mix Master (I recommend a Kitchen Aide® Stand Mixer)
> ➢ Muffin Pans, Cookie Sheets, Bundt Pan,
> ➢ Donut Pan
> ➢ Measuring cups/spoons
> ➢ Parchment paper
> ➢ Non Stick Spray (make sure there are no dairy proteins!)

These should only be used to make GF/CF items. This eliminates the possibility of cross contamination.

Flour

You must always have an ample supply of GF/CF flour on hand. I make it by the container full and here is a quick way of mixing the necessary flours. Mix these flours in an airtight container – the flour will be ready when you are!

3 lbs. White Rice Flour
2 lbs. Potato Starch Flour
1 lb. Tapioca Flour

Note: There are other GF/CF flours available on the market. You can choose soy flour, bean flours (which add protein), sweet rice flour, and brown rice flour. The above flour mix is what I found to taste most like regular wheat flours. Feel free to experiment with other flours to get different textures and flavors.

Xantham Gum or Guar Gum

This is a necessary ingredient in GF/CF baking. This is what replaces the gluten to give baked goods their dough like texture – if you forget to add it, your items will crumble.

Add 1 tsp. of xantham gum per cup of GF/CF flour mix above

Baking Powder and Vanilla

These are two necessary ingredients for baking that surprised me with a gluten factor.

Baking Powders sold in the regular grocery store may contain wheat flour as an anti-caking agent and vanilla may be extracted with a wheat-based alcohol. Make sure that you get recommended vanilla brands found at health food stores as well as GF/CF baking powder.

Semi-Sweet Chocolate Chips!

Chocolate Chip cookies are a child's right! In the recipe section of this book, there are two different recipes. Each makes a large batch of cookies so you are not always baking. If you are on a tight budget, use only half a bag of chocolate chips instead of the whole bag to stretch out the chocolate chips.

The chips also make great little chocolate snacks. When other kids are eating M&M's®, your child can have a chocolate treat, too. I also melt them and use candy forms to make suckers and candy shapes.

> HINT: The chocolate chip cookie recipes make a lot of cookies. If you do not need the whole batch, or just do not have time to bake them all, roll them into small balls and freeze them. When you need more cookies, it is just as convenient as the store ready-to-bake cookie dough.

Chapter 4

Meals

Breakfast

Thanks to the health conscientiousness of the population, GF/CF food is easier to find. There are lots of good cereals that kids love. Some of our favorites are Barbara's Organic Brown Rice Crisps®, Enviro Kidz brand including a Koala Crisp®, Gorilla Munch®, Frosted Flakes and Panda Puffs®.

You can use Barbara's Rice Crisps with soy butter and GF/CF marshmallows, and make a great rice crispy treat! (See recipe.)

Waffles and Pancakes are a sumptuous breakfast. There are good frozen waffles which most health food stores (and even some major grocery chains) carry. There are also a variety of ready made mixes – just add eggs and water to make delicious pancakes and waffles. If you do not have one of these mixes mix on hand, try my recipe to whip up your own homemade pancakes and waffles. Make extra and freeze for use during the week. I even prepackage my own dry ingredients. Then during the week when I am pressed for time, I can quickly add eggs and dairy free milk and whip up some fresh pancakes!

Syrup of choice should be the real thing – Maple Syrup, no additives and a delightful taste. Use sparingly as it has a high sugar content.

HINT: Both frozen waffles and pancakes taste better if you defrost them in the microwave instead of toasting them. They are moister and taste more like the real deal.

There are many web-sites that have lists of brands and ingredients that help you make good decisions. Some have ingredient books and other helpful materials for purchase and others offer links to find ingredients on line – see Appendix for web site lists and descriptions. There are also many other pre-made items that are good for breakfast as well. From chocolate and blueberry muffins to cinnamon rolls in the freezer section to the dry aisle section where you can find quick mixes to make muffins, scones and cranberry bread. Always check all the ingredients. Remember that Wheat Free does not necessarily mean Gluten Free or Casein Free!

Lunches

If your child is off to school, the school cafeteria will offer them little – most lunch menus are loaded with wheat, dairy and high fat/fried foods. The best bet is to get your child used to sandwiches and maybe some soup.

The favorite at our house is the classic PBJ (peanut butter and jelly). We use real peanut butter and squeezable jellies (so the rest of the family does not double dip the knife!).

Small bags of gf chips or pretzels, a piece of fruit or carrots will make a well balanced lunch.

If your child yearns for an Oscar Mayer® Lunchable, make your own! Ideas and recipes are in the back.. A GF/CF cookie is always a special treat.

Dinner

Believe it or not, most of what you probably make for dinner can be modified to be GF/CF or may actually be GF/CF without trying!

Obviously fried chicken and mashed potatoes are not acceptable choices, but baked chicken and baked potatoes are just fine. Just make sure you use dairy free margarine.

Rice is a staple in my family. Making a grilled a steak or a pot roast adds no gluten. If you use flour as a thickener in your own recipes, use corn starch instead.

I have included dinner ideas and recipes to help you feed your entire family without making two meals.

Pasta

There are many varieties of pasta that are wheat free. Corn pasta and Quinoa Pastas are firmer and less soggy that some of the rice or potato pastas. Experiment and see which one your child likes.

> HINT: Be careful not to overcook the pasta – it gets soggy. Add a drop of olive oil to the boiling water to help prevent sticking.

Again, cheese or any type of Parmesan topping is generally prohibited. There are soy versions, but most of them contain casein. Check the labels.

If you would like to top it off with sauce, remember to check the label. I would avoid sauces with high fructose corn syrup as I find these to make my daughter hyper-active. Stick to organic marinara sauces and make sure there are no added cheese products or whey.

Saturday Night Pizza

Let's face it – everyone loves pizza. Unfortunately, from the hand tossed wheat crust to the gooey mozzarella topping, regular pizza is not a reality on a GF/CF diet.

Do not dismay, however, as there are ways to get around this. If you are starting your child on the diet at a young age, the GF/CF way will be how they think pizza should be! If you are trying to start this with an older child, one who already loves the cheesy, crispy, stuffed crust version, this will be a little more challenging.

You can make your own pizza crust, or go the easy way – Kinnikinnick™ foods makes the most awesome personal pan size crusts. They come 4 to a package and make pizza making easy.

Although I do not use any cheese on my daughter's pizza, I use a wonderful, flavorful organic pizza sauce made by Muir Glen®. Spread pizza sauce on the crust and bake in a toaster oven until slightly brown.

I am hoping in the future to begin adding veggies, but since she is so texture oriented now, we stick to just the sauce and crust. Recently, Italian sausage has become a favorite. Grill or broil a link of the sausage and cut it up, then mix it with the sauce – it makes a yummy sausage pizza!

HINT: Make this an activity that you and your child to do together. Let them help prepare toppings. Ask them if they would like to try sautéed mushrooms or green peppers in olive oil! Let them make it their own creation!

Desserts

In my opinion, no life is complete without dessert. In my interaction with many parents who are doing the diet with their children, many just have eliminated dessert. I believe that dessert is not only a favorite food, but a social component as well. Let's face it, how many times do you get together with friends for cake and coffee. Will your child be the only one without dessert at a friend's party?

To help my daughter join in celebrations with peers at school, she always has a bag with her special snacks available to choose from.

Although she knew she could not have the cream filled chocolate frosted cupcake someone brought in for their birthday, she could go to her special treat bag and pick out something. These treats included candy that was GF/CF, cookies, brownies and chocolates that were dairy free.

I love to bake, so making special cakes, donuts, cookies and cupcakes are never a problem. Manufacturers seem to be aware of many of the food allergies and are now labeling their food and even taking gluten and casein out of their foods along with trans-fats and other unhealthy additives. This makes it easier to find prepared foods that are delicious.

Keep in mind that many daycare centers need to have prepackaged unopened foods to comply with health department codes. There are many prepackaged cookies, donuts, cinnamon rolls and muffins that make this task easy.

Snacks

Snacks are relatively simple. There are many ready to purchase snacks that are okay. Tortilla chips, potato chips and corn chips are acceptable snacks. Watch for the flavored chips or chips in the cans, as they often contain wheat flour. Whenever possible, stay away from hydrogenated oils. These are not good for anyone, but the less processed the ingredients the better.

Pretzels were the one thing off the list. This was a very difficult snack to give up. There are several tasty brands available at most health food stores. EnerG® makes a great mini pretzel. Many health food stores let you buy items by the case. This may be a great way to cut some costs if you find your child has a favorite.

Unfortunately, goldfish-shaped crackers are no longer an option and there is no replacement. I have found a few recipes, but they are time consuming and since cheese is the hardest on the diet to replace, you are probably better off eliminating it altogether. EnerG® makes a good saltine like cracker which we used with peanut butter or in our homemade Lunchable. You can make s'mores with them, as well. I recently discovered that Kinnikinnick® Foods now has a graham style cracker called "S'moreables." This has made sitting around our fire pit so much more fun. My daughter can make her own s'mores using her special ingredients.

Puddings and Gelatin – Although there are some warnings of food colorings, etc. in gelatin, I find this overall to be a tasty treat. Again, if you find your child obsesses about this snack, it probably is not good for him/her, but once or twice a week as a lunch snack is probably okay. Pudding is obviously a no-no due to the milk, but there are some mixes available by Imagine® that you can make with soy milk or Vance's DairiFree™. To the regular palette, these puddings may not taste the same as real chocolate pudding, however, to those used to a GF/CF diet, this pudding can be a satisfying treat.

What else can I feed my child?

There are many websites that can help you navigate this diet. See the appendix at the end of the book.

What else do I do in my own family? I cook gluten-free in most of my recipes. Meatloaf? I use corn meal. Soups? I purchase GF soup base and use fresh chicken.

Hamburger, Oscar Mayer™ or Boars Head™ lunch meats as well as plain old chicken are the favorite meats in my house. White Rice is always a perfect side dish. There are many marinades and salad dressings that are GF, or you can make your own.

Fresh and frozen produce are a must for any well balanced diet. Freeze Green Grapes and they are just like candy! Baby carrots with peanut butter (if no allergies are present) are also a healthy after school snack. I also always keep Asian pears, mangos, and star fruit as a quick pick-me-up before dinner.

Apples and Apple Juice, Bananas and Red Grapes

I suggest you remove apples and apple juice from your child's diet immediately.

My daughter would eat apples by the bagfuls and drink juice by the gallons. I thought it was healthy! Well, it turns out that she is highly sensitive to the phenol sulfates that naturally occur in the fruits. Her behavior changes radically the minute she consumes any apples or juice – even juice blends with apples as an ingredient.

Instead, we use Asian pears, red pears and Bartlett pears. She enjoys peaches and melon as well. Orange juice, pear juice and white grape juice are good juice substitutes. Water is always a good choice as well.

Eating Out

If you are going to eat out, there are many options. If you are going to just a little corner restaurant or a chain restaurant, order a burger with no bun, or ask if the chef can grill a piece of chicken with a little salt and pepper in some olive oil. You always run the risk of contamination when eating out, but I have found those foods to be okay, in general. You can purchase enzymes which help break down gluten and casein, so if you are unsure, you can always have your child take one before or after a meal.

Pasta places are much more difficult to navigate for your GF/CF child. However, I have found places like Maggiano's Little Italy (A Lettuce Entertain You Restaurant) offers gluten free pasta. They even made her new red sauce so there was no chance of it containing cheese or flour. One of our local Italian places also offers gluten free pasta. If you are dining out for pizza, you will have to make the pizza ahead of time and take it with you. Most restaurants are happy to provide a plate for her special food.

When dining at fast food restaurants, it is important to be aware of ingredients used in food preparation. I used to think that the grilled chicken offerings were fine. McDonald's® grilled chicken was one of her favorites. She would gobble it up like no tomorrow! Then I noticed the addiction pattern. She would tell me she "needed" chicken for dinner. The hand flapping started, and I knew something was not right. The nutrition information indicated the chicken is made with milk and wheat flour. Always check the ingredients. Beware of the new KFC grilled chicken as well. It has wheat and dairy flavorings and although it is delicious, it is not the right choice for someone on the GF/CF diet.

French Fries are another culprit in the fast food industry. Many fries are flavored or coated with spices which mean they contain modified food starch made from wheat. Just be watchful and ask. Many restaurants have nutrition guides somewhere on their walls. If you are not sure, just check. They also may fry other foods with wheat coatings. This can contaminate the oil and pass the gluten into otherwise gluten free foods.

Chapter 5

A Little About Biomedical Research

The diet does not do it all. You need a comprehensive plan to suit your child's needs. My belief is that the diet opened pathways to my daughter's brain making it possible for her to learn easier.

She seemed to respond better to all her therapies and many of her sensitivities and autistic behavior have subsided since the diet. I want to stress, however, that we have worked closely with a doctor who provides care for the "biomedical" side of the equation.

We provide our daughter daily with supplements like DMG, 5HTP, Methyl-B12, Calcium, Zinc, L-Glutathione and selenium. We also use homeopathic treatments to help her levels of heavy metals and levels of immunity from vaccines.

My recommendation is that you look to see if there is a doctor in your area who provides services for these alternative approaches. DO NOT, *I REPEAT*, DO NOT go to the health food store and start randomly picking out supplements to try on your child. In addition to the diet, my daughter had hair testing for heavy metals and blood work done to test her immune system.

Also, if you plan on working with your doctor or pediatrician, be prepared. Many traditional physicians do not believe that the diet works. I was once at an Autism conference where a doctor was going over all the pharmaceutical drug therapies that are available. When I asked about the diet, he told me there were no medical studies proving the diet has any impact, but if it made me "feel better", it would not do any harm to my child.

Believe me, this is not an easy task. I do not do this to make myself "feel better". Ask any parent who has seen the change in their child, even if it is only slight, and they will tell you that it is worth it.

You will probably come across many nay-sayers while pursuing this type of treatment. Watch your child and persevere. For many children on the spectrum, the diet, the supplements and alternative therapies may not have an effect – but for many they do, and it is certainly worth trying. Every day I watch my little girl play with friends, do her school work and work hard at living in the everyday world. Her autistic tendencies are still ever present, and we work each day to manage her emotions, her learning style and her interaction with her peers. It is exhausting on some days and very rewarding on most. Yet, we can go to the mall, to the movies and out to dinner. There was a time when I could not leave the house without a tantrum looming in the distance. If the activity was not on the picture schedule, it was not going to happen that day. Life has smoothed out so much with the help of therapists, teachers, support groups, family and for me, my faith.

You need to be diligent in your search for those therapists and doctors that will work with your child. Be honest with teachers, daycare providers and family as to how you are working with your child and what you are doing. You will often second guess yourself. Don't. You are taking steps to help your child, and even if you don't find success in everything you try, at least you know that you have tried.

Chapter 6

Opinions and Advice

I am not a medical doctor. I admit that some of the things I have tried for my daughter some may consider voodoo! She sees a chiropractor on a regular basis as I believe that when the spine is aligned, the body works better. We have used meditation, massage, and Reiki to calm her in her younger years. I have tried scented calming oils and candles. I set up my own play therapy in the basement of my house and taught her how to play and pretend. I have enlisted the help of her friends and their parents when she has attended parties and play dates.

We used to live our lives according to a picture schedule. If it was not on the schedule, it was not going to happen. Composing social stories was a part of my new job description. We had one for going to the doctor, one for going shopping. We even had to make special stories for expected behavior in school and even a special one for the amusement park and vacations.

As my daughter got older, picture schedules were replaced by word schedules. But each and every day we had to spell out what was happening. We ran our lives by an egg timer. Since the concept of time was hard for her to understand, I would just set a timer to help her make those transitions. Today, she can tell time and keeps her own schedule. I wake her up for school and she programs her morning from there. She cannot easily dress if she has not had breakfast, and her grooming routine is always in the same order. She still likes certain fabrics and colors, although will try more things than before. We still build in transition breaks, but it helps keep life running smoothly.

We are now beginning to enter uncharted waters known as puberty. As her body develops and her interests begin to focus on more grown-up activities, I feel the slippery slope. Her maturity, however, amazes me and through all her therapies and lessons, she has become a superb communicator. I believe that communication is the answer to help control their frustrations and tantrums from their younger years. If we help our children with Autism to express their frustrations in ways other than screaming and tantrums, I believe we hold the key to helping them grow and develop.

I also want to stress that I feel blessed, as my daughter has responded well to all we have tried and has High Functioning Autism. She walks the tightrope line between the Autistic World and the "Normal" World and sometimes just jumps off for a while when she can.

"Planet Yahoo" is what she calls her escape. I often see her go there when the room is over-stimulating or the homework too hard. Even her teachers have made comments on her quick little trips. She will often laugh to herself, smile and just seem to be in a really enjoyable place. I think most of us are slightly envious of the ability to escape so easily. She is constantly reminded to stay with us, stay focused. Only with the promise to slip away at a later time, does she come back to be with us.

With the combination of diet, therapy and supplements as well as constant family support, I believe that my daughter is on her way to living a full rich life and becoming a contributing member of society. As I write this, she is "working" as a Counselor-in-Training for a camp she used to attend. No longer a camper, she works with younger children who she says remind her of herself when she was that age. To watch her help other children cope with their everyday lives is truly progress!

In conclusion......

Well, there may never be a finish line for you or your child...but it does get easier. Teach your GF/CF child how to eat. Explain that the reason you are taking away foods is because you found out that sickness may occur if the wrong foods are eaten. Your child will understand. After he/she has been off the foods for a while, if your child accidentally ingests wheat or dairy, he or she may not feel well and may experience stomach cramps, diarrhea, or edginess.

This theory was put to the test in my home. She has been a Girl Scout for three years. On one occasion, they had an event that included all the Girl Scout Troops in the surrounding area. It was called a "Tasting Tea" and each troop chose to showcase scouting from another country. The troops made food to go along with their country's display. The girls got a chance to taste all the foods. My daughter asked (okay, begged) me to let her taste whatever she wanted. I agreed. When I picked her up, she told me all of the foods she had tasted. Many of the sweets made with flour, butter and milk. She seemed happy and perky and I thought that maybe we had reached a point where gluten and casein did not matter so much. Boy, were we wrong!

In the continuing hours of that day, she began hair twirling (her new stim when she let her hair grow out). By evening, she was totally zoned out on the couch watching the same show she had watched earlier that day. When I asked her if she was okay, she spoke in a monotone voice and told me, "Mom, I don't care about anything, anymore." I was so startled by this announcement of the way she was feeling that I asked her why she thought she felt that way. She answered, in that monotone voice, "Because I ate wheat."

Well, it took almost three days to get it out of her system. She takes an enzyme called EnZymAid™* which is made by Kirkman Labs. It is a plant-based enzyme complex that specifically targets the breakdown of casein and gluten (www.kirkmanlabs.com). For my daughter, it was a reality check on how she feels when she eats foods containing gluten and casein.

I hope that the following recipe section will give you a quick start and the confidence to try this diet. There are so many more food allergies and intolerances in this realm of special diets, but I have gone directly to addressing gluten and casein. If your child cannot have eggs, there is an egg replacer that can be used instead. It is made by EngerG® Foods.

Peanut butter is a staple for my daughter and I am so grateful she can eat it, but many children are allergic to peanuts. There are delicious soy butters out there that may work instead of peanut butter.

I have found many more foods available in regular supermarkets that are acceptable. Ghirardelli makes a wonderful dark chocolate square that has no casein. Do a Google search for GF/CF foods and you will find links to all kinds of GF/CF foods that you can have delivered right to your home.

If you have favorite recipes, make a few quick substitutions on your own and you can still enjoy it. Have heart and do not give up. It is okay if a few things end up in the garbage along the way. Try and not think of this diet as a hardship, but as an adventure. Good luck in the kitchen!

A note about the Enzyme. I have met people in my journey who use the enzyme so that their child can eat wheat. I do not recommend this. The build up of the proteins seems to happen quickly. I recommend using the enzyme to handle mistakes, not entire meals. Contact your doctor if you have specific questions.

LET'S GET COOKING!

Index of Recipes:

GFCF Flour Mix:

Here is one of the most important things for GF/CF Cooking – the Flour mix. You can get these specialty flours at your local health food store as well as many major food chains in the special aisles with Soy Milk, organic cereals, etc. I order my flour from Barry Foods, listed in the appendix at the end of the book.

3 lbs. Rice Flour
2 lbs. Potato Starch Flour
1 lb. Tapioca Flour

Mix together – keep in airtight container and you are always ready to bake.

Don't forget to add <u>1 tsp. of Xantham Gum</u> for each cup of flour you use. Do this only when preparing a recipe – do not add into the above flour mix.

Breakfast

Waffles

1 ¼ Cups GF Flour Mix
1 Tsp. Xantham or Guar Gum
1 TBL sugar
4 Tsp. GF Baking Powder
½ tsp Salt

2 eggs
½ cup canola oil
1 ¾ cup of milk substitute*

Heat Waffle Iron
Mix together dry ingredients.
Beat eggs with hand beater or fork until fluffy.
Add eggs and oil to dry ingredients – mix.
Add milk substitute until batter is smooth.

Pour batter from cup or pitcher onto center of hot waffle iron, about ¼ cup.
Bake until steaming stops about 2-4 minutes. Remove waffle carefully.

Makes about 10 square waffles – let cool before freezing.

Use real Maple Syrup as it has no additives or corn syrup!

*add more or less to get batter to good consistency. Soy milk is thicker, so you may need to add a little water, but not too much, as it may become pasty. I prefer to use Vance's DariFree™

Pancakes

1 Cup GF Flour Mix
1 Tsp. Xantham or Guar Gum
3 tsp. GF Baking Powder
½ tsp Salt
1 TBLS Sugar

1 egg
2 TBLS of Canola Oil
1 Cup of milk substitute*

*add more or less to get batter to good consistency. Soy milk is thicker, so you may need to add a little water, but not too much as it may become pasty. I like to use Vance's™ DairiFree™.

Mix together dry ingredients
Beat egg with fork or hand whip until fluffy.
Add to dry ingredients, add milk until smooth (you may need to add a little more milk to get right consistency – it depends on what type of milk substitute you are using.)

Spray griddle or frying pan with non-stick canola oil – pour about 1/3 cup batter for each pancake. Cook pancakes until bubbly in the middle, then turn. Makes 12 pancakes.

You can add fresh blueberries to make blueberry pancakes.
Add dairy free chocolate chips to make fun chocolate chip pancakes!

Scrambled Eggs

Mix 2 eggs until frothy.

Melt a pat of Dairy Free Margarine in a small frying pan – add eggs.

As the egg mixture begins to set, lift the cooked portions and let the uncooked portions flow into the pan. Cook until eggs are thick but still moist.

Salt and pepper to taste.

You can add bacon (Oscar Meyer® center cut is the best) or ham (Oscar Meyer® and Boars Head® have no wheat fillers) to the eggs to make heartier scrambled eggs.

Blueberry Muffins

Preheat oven to 400°

2 Cups GF Flour Mix
2 Tsp. Xantham or Guar Gum
3 Tsp. GF Baking Powder
1 tsp Salt

¾ cup Milk Substitute
½ Cup Canola Oil
1 egg

1 Cup of Fresh Blueberries

Mix dry ingredients together.
Mix together wet ingredients.

Add eggs, milk and oil mixture to flour mix and stir well, adding a little more milk substitute as needed.

Fold in blueberries.

Divide mixture among muffin cups and sprinkle with a little sugar. Bake until golden brown, 18 to 20 minutes on a 400° oven.

Chocolate Chip Muffins

Replace 1 cup chocolate chips for 1 cup of Fresh Blueberries

Cereal

There are many brands of cereal you can give your child. Your health food store will have a selection of GF/CF cereals to choose from – just read the labels. Post® Fruity Pebbles and Cocoa Pebbles are also free of wheat and gluten. Beware of the generic brands as they may have fillers.

Remember, just because the front of the box says they are a Rice or Corn Cereal, read the labels – often times they contain barley, or modified wheat starch.

Lunch Ideas!

When you have young children in school packing a lunch can be challenging. Most children with autism have lots of texture problems so fortunately, if you find something your child likes to eat for lunch, he/she may not have a problem eating the same lunch every day.

No Crust PBJ's

You have all seen the newest addition to the packaged take along lunch! These round, crustless Peanut butter and jelly sandwiches which are pre-packaged so you can just throw them in the lunch box, are every mom's dream.

Okay, so those with kids on the diet don't get to have it quite so convenient, but it is still possible to get that round, gooey jelly filled circle sandwich gluten free!

Take out 2 slices of GF bread from the freezer, defrost for 1 ½ minutes, then microwave for 20 seconds. You get two soft pieces of bread with that just baked feeling.

Spread on your favorite gluten free peanut butter or your favorite almond butter and jelly of choice. Although we have eliminated purple or red grapes from my daughter's diet, I have found that the teaspoon or so used of Welch's™ squeezable grape jelly has no effect on her behavior – so you may want to experiment. There are lots of jelly flavors to choose from, so you need to find your child's favorite!

Then, to make that perfectly round sealed sandwich I used a special tool which I purchased from the Pampered Chef® called the "Cut n Seal". It sells for about $10.00 and is a fun way to make crust less sandwiches.

Add some potato chips, a few carrots or some green grapes and you have a healthy, easy lunch, and your child's lunch won't look much different from the other kids!

Homemade Lunch in a Box!

Another lunch time phenomenon was the Oscar Mayer ™ Lunchable! This cute pre-packed lunch with little circles of ham, cheese, crackers, juice box and a special treat are many a parents' survival of that quick lunch that you don't have to pack.

Again, for us parents of kids on the diet, the convenience of these types of food is lost to us, but often time our kids want to feel special and have this unique lunch.

With a little time and effort your special diet child can have his or her own Lunchable™! Buy a container with special smaller dividers in it or buy a Lunchable™ – you eat the ingredients and save the container!

Take your child's favorite ham or turkey and cut the slices into circles with a small cookie or biscuit cutter. Forget the cheese since there is no good substitute. Then take the GF crackers or the small wheat free rice thins and put a stack of those in the container. Take lemonade or orange juice box and maybe a few cookies or a special dairy free chocolate treat. Imagine the delight when your child opens his/her lunch to find a Lunchable™! I am sure your child will be the envy of the other kids at the table.

Sandwiches

If your child doesn't get hung up on the fancy crust less sandwiches or lunch in a box, a good old fashioned sandwich may be just the ticket.

Again, Kinnikinnick® Foods White Rice Bread is a thin sliced bread and is great for sandwiches. Choose lunch meats that are free from wheat fillers and add mayo or mustard to taste.

Hot Dogs

Another lunch favorite is the hot dog. Oscar Meyer or Vienna™ all beef Hot Dogs (watch ingredients closely) are a staple in my fridge. If you go out, most hot dog stands (especially in Chicago) have the Vienna™ All beef and we just order it without the bun.

At home, you can order Hot Dog buns from Kinnikinnick™ Foods – defrost for 2 minutes, microwave high for 30 seconds and you have a warm steamed bun – add your child's favorite condiments and enjoy.

Hamburgers

There is no change to this all American lunch or dinner – When going out, just order the hamburger without the bun. At home a juicy grilled burger is always a summer treat. Kinnikinnick™ has a great GFCF Hamburger bun that creates a wonderful treat. Load it up with GF ketchup or some lettuce and tomatoes and your child has a tasty treat.

Note: Watch out for boxed hamburgers that are already seasoned – they often have flavoring that contain wheat or wheat fillers – best to stick with 100% ground beef.

Homemade French Fries

Just peel a potato, cut up into fry shapes and deep fry in canola oil! If you don't have a deep fryer just take a small frying pan and heat up some canola oil. Once hot, place a shallow layer of fries into the pan and cook until golden brown.

A note on restaurant French Fries.

In the early stages, you must avoid cross contamination as much as possible. Restaurants often fry other, wheat coated foods in the oil they cook their fries in. Ask the restaurant if they use the oil for any other foods. Once your child has been on the diet for a while, they may not be sensitive to small amounts – you just have to watch behavior. I have always found McDonald's® French fries okay.

Chicken Salad

This one will definitely be an acquired taste – definitely for the older, less tactile taste bud – but even those on a non GF-CF diet will love this salad.

2-3 boneless chicken breasts
Salt and pepper to taste
Splash of Olive Oil

1 Tbls. finely chopped onion
½ cup sliced green seedless grapes
¼ cup Mayonnaise

Place chicken in baking dish and bake in 350° oven with a little salt and pepper and a splash of olive oil until the chicken is white, but tender. Let cool. Cut chicken into cubes.

Mix the finely chopped onions, green grapes and mayonnaise with chicken cubes. Mix together using more or less mayo to taste. Stuff in a tomato or just eat plain with a few GF crackers and you have a nice light lunch.

Hint: When you make the chicken breasts, bake a few extra, slice into cubes and freeze so you will have some ready in a jiffy. Market Day™ also makes pre-cooked chicken pieces that are freezer ready and easy to use.

Dinner Ideas

This is when the GF/CF diet can either be the hardest or easiest! Many of the foods you already make are GF/CF, but if you have a picky eater, you will find yourself making two meals each night. Parties can be especially hard. In this section, I have tried to give you a variety of recipes that you can make for the whole family and that your GF/CF child will enjoy as well.

As every child is different, tactile senses to different meats may be a problem. For instance, my daughter used to not like any kind of red meat unless it was ground. Although my pepper steak melts like butter, she did not like the texture of this meat. Now, she breaks the bank at a restaurant savoring prime rib! You will have to try out the different recipes to see what your child likes best – and you can always make a double batch and freeze individual portions so on the night the rest of you are not eating GF/CF, you can just defrost and heat a single serving of a favorite food.

Stuffed Peppers
(Makes about 4 peppers)

1 lb. ground beef
1 cup rice (not instant)
¼ cup finely chopped onion
Salt/pepper to taste
4 small green peppers with tops cut off and seeded.
1 large can tomatoes

Mix ground beef, rice, onion, salt and pepper in a bowl.

Make 4 balls of meat and "stuff" into cut open peppers.
Place in pressure cooker. Pour tomatoes over stuff peppers and add water to cover. Seal lid of cooker.

After pressure cooker begins to jiggle- use 10 lbs. of pressure -cook about 15 minutes.

You can make this a slow cooker as well. Add ingredients and add water to cover – cook 3-4 hours on high or 5-6 hours on low.

"Garbage"

When I was growing up and watched my mom make this recipe, we used to ask her what she was making, and she would say "garbage"!

Basically, this is pepper steak with whatever extra veggies you want to throw in it!

1 round steak cut into serving pieces
1 medium onion, wedged
7 or 8 - 3" pieces of celery
1 green pepper, seeded and cut into chunks
2 Whole Tomatoes, chunked (or a 14 oz. can of diced tomatoes)
1 tsp. allspice (ground or whole)
1 tsp. oregano

In pressure cooker pot, brown meat in a little olive oil on both sides, sprinkle with salt and pepper. Add other ingredients, sprinkle with oregano over the top. Add water to cover.

Cook 30 minutes after weight begins to jiggle. Use 10 lbs. of pressure.

If you don't have or like to use a pressure cooker, then you can use a slow cooker. Brown the meat on stove top and then place in slow cooker. Add all the ingredients, add water to cover and cook on high for 3-5 hours or low for 6-8 hours.

Meatloaf

A family favorite, especially if you are on a budget.

1 lb. ground meat (either beef or turkey)
1 lb. ground pork
1 small onion diced
½ cup GF/CF Bread crumbs or corn meal
1 egg, slightly beaten
Salt/pepper to taste

Mix all ingredients together and form a loaf.
Place in a loaf pan and cover with a small can of tomato sauce.
Bake at 350° for 30 minutes.

You can also make this in a slow cooker, although it won't get brown on top. Bake at low for 5-6 hours and high for 3-4 hours. Make sure you fill the bottom of the pan with water.

Seasoned Chicken

Baked chicken is always a favorite in my house. Whether it is boneless or bone in chicken, baking a cut up chicken seasoned with your favorite spices is always a sure bet.

If you are baking a whole chicken, rub with olive oil and then season with salt, pepper and poultry spices. Place in shallow roasting pan. Add about 1 cup of water to the bottom of the pan, cover and bake at 350° for an hour. I add celery and carrots and onion slices around the chicken to add extra flavor.

I have a wonderful stoneware cooker (like the ones you can get from The Pampered Chef®) that makes moist, tender chicken. Remember, you cannot stuff this chicken – if your family enjoys stuffing, you can make it on the side.

Baked Chicken Pieces

For cut up chicken, rub a little olive oil into the skin of each piece and salt and pepper to taste. Arrange in baking dish.

Add other favorite spices – Italian or spicy. You can also brush with a little GF/CF BBQ sauce. Add green peppers, onions, celery or carrots – whatever suits you and bake at 350° for 30-45 minutes until juices run clear.

Chinese Chicken

A quick, easy recipe!

4 boneless chicken breasts-cubed
1 small onion, chopped
2 stalks celery chopped
1 cup frozen green beans
1 can water chestnuts
1 can bean sprouts or fresh bean sprouts
1/3 cup wheat free Tamari* sauce
4 TBLS of canola oil
1 cup GF Chicken Broth

In a large frying pan or wok, heat the oil and sauté the chicken until white – drain. Add onions and celery and sauté until clear. Then add green beans, water chestnuts and 1/3 cup Tamari sauce and sauté for a few more minutes. Add broth and cook until tender (about 10-12 minutes). Add the bean sprouts and heat through. Serve over white rice.

Do not use Soy Sauce – although the name says "soy", the key ingredient is also wheat. I use San-J® organic Tamari Sauce that is guaranteed gluten free.

For a quick change, substitute the chicken with cooked, peeled and deveined shrimp for Chinese Shrimp!

Pork Roast with Pears

Pork Roast or Pork Tenderloin
Salt/Pepper
½ tsp. Rosemary
2 pears, peeled and halved (fresh or canned)

Rinse pork and pat with salt and pepper.
Place in baking dish and sprinkle with Rosemary.
Place pears around the roast – add about 1 cup of water to bottom of pan.

Bake at 350° until meat thermometer reads 170 °.
Slice and serve with a tossed salad and rice.

Grilled Tilapia or Salmon

4-6 pieces of Tilapia or Salmon steaks.

Prepare a foil packet – spray with nonstick spray.

Place fish in packet and drizzle with olive oil. Add spice of your choice – I love the Cajun spice, but you can use lemon pepper or garlic salt.

Close up the packet and grill or bake until fish separates easily.

Pasta

1 cup cooked, any type of GF pasta
1 cup red sauce (Look for canned sauces that do not contain any cheeses or flour thickeners. Marinara is usually the best)
2-3 Italian sausage

Cook pasta and drain.

Remove skin from sausage and break up in small frying pan and cook until done.

Mix with favorite pasta sauce and pour over pasta.

GF Meatballs

1 lb. ground beef
¼ cup corn meal or GF bread crumbs
1 egg
Salt and Pepper to taste

Mix together all of the above. Make into round meatballs, any size. Place on baking sheet lined with parchment paper.

Bake at 400° for 20 minutes.

Serve with pasta or just red sauce on a GF hotdog bun for a meatball sandwich.

Homemade Chicken Soup

3 boneless chicken breasts
3 stalks celery
1 onion quartered
8 cups of water
4 tsp. or 4 cubes GF chicken base
1 tsp. allspice
1 tsp. basil
1 tsp. oregano
1 tsp sea salt

Place all ingredients into large soup pot and simmer for 30-40 minutes until chicken is done.

Remove chicken pieces and dice into small pieces. Strain soup of all veggies and spices. Add chicken and additional salt and pepper to taste. Serve with GF noodles or white rice.

This soup freezes great – so double the recipe and you will always have soup ready!

Red Hot Chili

2 – 16 oz cans of Dark Red Kidney Beans (drained)
2 – 14 oz cans of diced or crushed tomatoes
2 lbs ground meat, browned and drained (you can use ground turkey or beef)
2 medium onions chopped
1 green pepper chopped
2 cloves of garlic, crushed
2-3 tables of chili powder
1 tsp. of cumin
Salt and pepper to taste.

Put all ingredients in crock pot. Stir. Cook low 10-12 hours, or high 5-6 hours. You may also cook on the stovetop – 2-3 hours medium heat – add water as needed.

Spanish Rice

1 cup of long grain rice
1 cup of canola oil
Small onion – diced
¼ cup tomato sauce
1 clove of garlic or pinch of garlic powder
2 cups of water
1 cube or 1 tsp of GF chicken base

Rinse rice in warm water and soak for 10 minutes. In sauce pan, heat the oil and add the drained rice. Fry the rice, onion, and garlic together for about 5 minutes. Drain the oil.

Add tomato sauce, water, chicken base, and salt to taste. Cover and let simmer until the rice absorbs all the water. (about 15-18 minutes)

Be careful not to burn the rice. Serve as a side dish to your favorite meal.

This rice can be tricky – you need to make sure you soak it, and don't fry it too hard, or your rice can be soggy or crunchy. If you accidentally burn the rice, take a damp paper towel and place it over the rice. Cover and let sit for about 5 minutes. The towel absorbs the burnt taste. It works well on plain white rice as well.

Tacos

1 lb. ground beef browned, or
3 boneless chicken breasts baked and shredded

1 can of diced tomatoes with hot Chile peppers

Salt and Pepper to taste.

Mix browned ground beef or shredded chicken with tomatoes and salt and pepper in a frying pan.

Stir until all ingredients are mixed and warmed through.

Serve on hard corn taco shells or soft corn tortillas that have been warmed in the microwave for 35 -50 seconds.

Add fresh sliced lettuce and extra tomato chunks for flavor.
Serve with Spanish Rice.

Desserts

Chocolate Chip Cookies (#1)

1 cup canola oil
1 cup CF margarine (softened)
2 eggs
1 cup sugar
1 cup brown sugar
2 tsp. GF Vanilla
1 tsp. Baking Soda
1/2 tsp. salt
4 cups GF Flour Mix
4 tsp. Xantham Gum
1 bag CF Chocolate chips

In mix master bowl, beat oil, margarine and sugar until fluffy. Add eggs and vanilla. Sift dry ingredients together and add to wet mixture slowly. Blend well (I recommend high for 2-3 minutes). Stir in chocolate chips.

Drop dough on baking sheet lined with parchment paper by rounded tablespoons. Press down with fingers to flatten cookies. Bake at 350 for 10-12 minutes. Place on cookie rack to cool.

Makes about 4 dozen cookies

Note: GF/CF cookies are a little more fragile until cooled. Store in plastic container with lid – you may also freeze.

Chocolate Chip Cookies (#2)
(These are more cake-like cookies)

1 lb. CF margarine, softened
6 eggs slightly beaten
1 cup sugar
1 cup brown sugar
2 tsp. GF Vanilla
2 tsp. Baking Soda
2 tsp. Baking Powder
1 tsp. salt
5 cups GF Flour Mix
5 tsp. Xantham Gum
1 bag CF Chocolate chips

In mix master bowl, beat margarine and sugar until fluffy. Add eggs and vanilla. Sift dry ingredients and blend well (I recommend high for 2-3 minutes). Stir in chocolate chips.

Drop dough on baking sheet lined with parchment paper by rounded teaspoons. Bake at 375 for 8-10 minutes.

Makes about 7 dozen cookies

Remember you can drop dough on foil, wax paper or parchment paper and freeze. Bake when you need them! Just make sure you store them in an airtight container.

You can also bake them and then freeze in freezer storage bag.

Peanut Butter Cookies

2 Eggs
2 Cups Peanut Butter
2 Cups Sugar

Mix together all ingredients. Shape into balls the size of walnuts and place on cookie sheet lined with parchment paper. Bake in preheated 375 oven for 10 minutes. Take a fork dipped in sugar and press a criss-cross pattern into each cookie. Bake for 1 minute more.

Remove from pan, cool.

To add a chocolate treat, instead of criss-crossing cookies with fork, press in 3 dairy free chocolate chips and bake for 1 more minute.

Makes about 5 dozen cookies.

Spritz Cookies

1 cup CF margarine, softened
½ cup sugar
2 ¼ cups CF Flour mix, sifted
2 tsp. Xantham Gum
½ tsp. salt
1 egg
1 tsp. CF Vanilla Extract

Heat oven to 400°. Cream together margarine and sugar. Add remaining ingredients. Beat for about 2 minutes.

Place dough in cookie press, and put cookies on parchment lined cookie sheet. Bake for 6-9 minutes – watch so they don't get too brown.

For fancy decorated cookies, sprinkle with colored sugar. You can purchase raw sugar and tint with food coloring to make your own!

Immediately remove to cooling rack. Makes about 5 dozen.

Crisp Rice Treats

30 Large GF Marshmallows (recommend Kraft Jet Puffed®)
¼ cup of CF margarine
½ tsp GF vanilla
5 cups GF Crisp Rice Cereal

Heat marshmallows and margarine in large saucepan on low heat until smooth.

Add vanilla and cereal until well coated.

Press into a 9x9 pan which has been sprayed with canola oil.

Let cool, cut into bars, about 2x1. Yields about 36 bars.

S'mores

Roast 1 GF/CF large marshmallow until done.
Place on ½ GF cracker. Sprinkle on a few CF chocolate chips.
Place other half of GF cracker and press together!

Cakes with Frosting

To make an easy birthday cake, my favorite cake mix is made by the Really Great Food Company®. It is a box cake that can be made into two loaf cakes, 4 8x8 cakes, 1 bundt pan, or two 9" layer cakes.

It freezes wonderfully, so you can pick and choose which way you want to make it and for what occasion.

The GF/CF frosting I use is Betty Crocker® white frosting. Although it has more additives than I usually like to use, such as corn syrup and modified corn starch, for the occasional special cake, I see no harm in using it. If you are creative, you can use food coloring and a cake decorator to make fancy shapes and designs and make a one of a kind cake for your child.

If, however, you want to try your hand at baking your own cakes, try my yellow cake recipe to follow.

Donuts and Cupcakes

Again, using a pre-packaged cake mix, you can make donuts, large or small, simply by purchasing special donut baking pans available in your local kitchen stores. It's a fun way to add a little variety to your child's desserts, and they can be easily frozen in individual baggies.

Brownies

There are some really great box mixes that make terrific GF/CF brownies. Peruse your local store and find the one that your child loves best. If you don't have time to bake, look for ready made brownies in the GF/CF aisle.

Yellow Cake

2 cups GF Flour Mix
2 tsp. Xantham Gum
1 ½ cups sugar
½ cup CF margarine
1 cup prepared DariFree® Milk
3 ½ tsp. of GF baking powder
1 tsp salt
1 tsp. GF Vanilla
3 eggs, slightly beaten

Heat oven to 350°. Grease and flour with GF/CF margarine and flour, a 13x9x2 pan or 2 round pans for a layer cake.

Sift flour, xantham gum, baking powder and salt in separate bowl. Cream together margarine and sugar. Add eggs and vanilla. Alternate dry ingredients and dairy free milk. Beat on high 3 minutes.

Pour into pan and bake 40-45 minutes or until toothpick inserted into middle of cake comes out clean. Cool and frost.

Asian Pear Frosting

This is a fun, whipped topping type of frosting that is easy to make.

1 egg white
1 cup sugar
1 Asian Pear- medium, peeled and grated

Put egg white into mixer and beat at high speed until egg starts to peak. Add sugar and continue beating – continuing to form small peaks. Add grated pear slowly and continue to beat mixture until it had a whipped cream type texture. When it holds its peaks, you can frost your cooled cake.

Marinades and Salad Dressings

There are many over the counter brands that are safe to use as marinades and salad dressings. Check out the web sites that offer GF/CF products and choose from their wide offerings. If you are in a pinch and need to make a quick Italian style dressing or marinade, here is one that you can always whip up in a jiffy.

Italian Marinade/Dressing

1 cup Canola Oil
¼ cup Rice Vinegar
2 Tbls. of chopped onion
1 tsp sugar
1 tsp. dried basil leaves
1 tsp. dried oregano
¼ tsp. black pepper
1 clove garlic, crushed
¼ tsp. crushed red pepper

Mix all ingredients in a covered container, pour over meat and refrigerate 2-4 hours. Great for grilled marinated chicken, pork chops or steaks. Refrigerate leftovers and used for salads.

BBQ Sauce

1 cup GF/CF Ketchup
½ small onion, chopped finely
1/3 cup water
¼ cup of CF margarine
1 Tbls. Paprika
1 tsp. brown sugar
½ tsp. salt
¼ tsp. pepper
¼ cup lemon juice
1 Tbls. Tamari sauce

Heat all ingredients expect lemon juice and tamari sauce, until boiling. Stir in lemon juice and Tamari sauce. Makes about 2 cups.

Breads and Rolls

For those of you who want a challenge, baking your own bread can be a true accomplishment. To follow is a recipe that, although time consuming, makes the best home-made bread or dinner rolls.

3 cups of GF Flour Mix
3 tsp. Xantham Gum
¼ cup sugar
½ cup Vance's DariFree® powder
1 tsp. unflavored gelatin
¾ tsp. Salt
1 tsp. honey
1 pkg. of dry active yeast
½ cup lukewarm water
¼ cup CF Margarine
1 ¼ cup water
1 tsp. Rice Vinegar
1 egg plus 1/3 cup + 1 Tbls. of liquid egg whites, beat together

Grease two loaf pans.

Sit flour, xantham gum and salt. Add milk powder, gelatin, and sugar. Blend well with regular beater.

Dissolve 2 tsp of sugar in ½ cup lukewarm water and add yeast. Let sit. Put water in saucepan with margarine and heat until melted.

Turn mixer on low and blend dry ingredients. Slowly add water, margarine and vinegar – blend well. Add egg and egg whites. Pour in yeast water and beat at highest speed for 4 minutes. The dough is more cake like than bread like, but don't be concerned.

Spray bread pans or muffin pans with non-stick spray. Put dough into loaf pans and let rise until doubled (about 40 minutes). Bake in pre-heated 400 oven for 40-50 minutes until brown and loaf sound hollow when tapped.

For rolls, place in muffin tins and let rise until doubled. Bake for about 25 minutes.

For added flavor you can brush the loaves or rolls with melted CF margarine.

Cut loaves with electric knife before freezing.

Natalie A Kulig

Pizza Crust

1 pkg. active dry yeast
1 cup warm water (105°to 115 °)
2 ½ cups GF Flour
2 tablespoons of canola oil
1 tsp. sugar
1 tsp. salt

Dissolve yeast in warm water. Stir together remaining ingredients. Add yeast; mix vigorously – about 20 strokes. Let rest 5 minutes. Roll out to 2 personal size pizza crusts or one large pizza.

Top with sauce and other toppings, bake in oven 400° oven 15-20 minutes.

62

Ingredients to Avoid

There are so many different types of additives to our foods these days, and it is mind boggling to keep up with them all. How many foods did you eat just today, that you really did not know what you were ingesting?

That morning cereal, you probably had Niacin amide, or Tricalcium Phosphate. Do we really know what they are or what they do? Probably not. Thank goodness the box says "CONTAINS WHEAT AND SOY INGREDIENTS". I do not have to look any farther.

That said, I want to try and give you the quick buzz words so that you know what to look for when purchasing foods. I have even taught my daughter to look for these so that she knows if she can have particular foods.

WHEAT

- All Purpose Flour
- Barley
- Graham
- Oat
- Rye
- Semolina
- Modified Food Starch (unless it says specifically corn, it is derived from wheat flour)
- Malt
- Spelt

DAIRY

- Lactose
- Magnesium Caseinate
- Caseinate
- Milk Fat
- Milk Solids
- Buttermilk Solids
- Whey

Other Suspect Ingredients

- Caramel color may also be suspect – watch your child's reaction if they had something with caramel coloring.
- Mono and dyglycerides – these may contain wheat, but can also be derived from corn. You may need to check with the manufacturer.
- MSG is safe as far as GF/CF, but not recommended.

Appendix

Sites you can purchase GF/CF Foods Direct:

www.kinnikinnick.com
Breads, baked goods – can arrange auto-shipment of your favorite items

www.ener-g.com
Snacks, Breads, flours, etc.

www.barryfarm.com
Flours, baking goods

Informational websites

www.gfcfdiet.com
Diet Information

www.gfco.org
Information about GF (pertains mostly to celiac so be careful as Celiacs don't have to eliminate dairy.)

www.autismndi.com
Autism Network for Dietary Interventions

www.kentuckiana.org
Specialized programs helping children with special needs.

Autism Websites

www.autism-society.org

Autism Society – First place to start your research and find out about autism as well as additional links and information

www.maapservices.org

MAAP Services for Autism and Asperger Syndrome is a nonprofit organization dedicated to providing information and advice to families of more advanced individuals with Autism, Asperger Syndrome and Pervasive Developmental Disorder (PDD).

Recommended Reading

Just as your child is unique, so are the books you may choose to read. Reading is my thing. I can take a book, devour it quickly and pick out information I think might work with my child. Even today and I try and devise study guides and tools to help my daughter study and cope with the "normal" world around her.

Below are just a few of my favorites which give help and insight to starting the diet plus other non-traditional ways you may want to help your child. Just go online and search "Autism" and an array of resources are at your finger tips. Choose wisely, do not overwhelm yourself. Be like a sifter – sort through the information, keep what appeals to you and discard the rest. You can always go back and pick up the information and start again.

The Child with Special Needs: Encouraging Intellectual Emotional Growth, Stanley Greenspan, Serena Wieder, Robin Simons, DaCapo Press, 1998.

Facing Autism: Giving Parents Reasons for Hope and Guidance for Help, Lynn M. Hamilton, Waterbrook Press, 2000.

Louder Than Words: A Mother's Journey in Healing Autism, Jenny McCarthy, Penguin Group (USA), 2007.

Ten Things Every Child with Autism Wishes You Knew, Ellen Natbohn, Future Horizons, 2005.

Thinking in Pictures and other reports from my Life with Autism, Temple Grandin, First Vintage Books, 1995.

Unraveling the Mysteries of Autism and Pervasive Development Disorder, Karyn Seroussi, Simon and Schuster, 2000.

Final Thoughts.....

There are many great cookbooks out there with tons of recipes. If this book seems a little slim on the recipe side, it is because I believe that some of the books are overwhelming.

Think about the cookbooks you have in your house right now – how many of those recipes do you actually use or have ever tried? Exactly! We all tend to be creatures of habit and find those handfuls of recipes that keep our families satisfied. This is what this book sets out to do. This book gives you the recipes to get you started and keep you going. When what your child eats begins to expand, start experimenting! Try making your favorite recipe gluten/casein free!

Remember, this is a life long choice. Keep it simple, make it fun and success will be yours.